This book is published strictly for historical purposes.
The Naval and Military Press Ltd
expressly bears no responsibility or liability of any type,
to any first, second or third party, for any harm,
injury or loss whatsoever.

The Naval & Military Press Ltd

Published by

The Naval & Military Press Ltd
Unit 5 Riverside, Brambleside
Bellbrook Industrial Estate
Uckfield, East Sussex
TN22 1QQ England

Tel: +44 (0)1825 749494

www.naval-military-press.com
www.nmarchive.com

*In reprinting in facsimile from the original, any imperfections are inevitably reproduced
and the quality may fall short of modern type and cartographic standards.*

IN REPLYING
REFER TO NO.

UNITED STATES MARINE CORPS
MARINE AVIATION DETACHMENT
NAVAL TRAINING SCHOOL (AVIATION)
NAVY PIER, CHICAGO, ILL.

Seldom before in American history has it been so necessary for the young men of America to be well trained in the science of physical fitness and combat conditioning. War today creates demands that were never before thought possible.

The armies of our enemies have been trained for years to prepare them for the struggle that they alone knew was coming—the struggle for which they alone are responsible. Make no mistake about it, they are tough.

America's problem today is to match and surpass the toughness of our enemies—and this can be done only through a thorough and far reaching program of physical training.

Our young men have the physical ability to adapt themselves for modern warfare through their training in High School and College of such sports as Football, Basket Ball, Wrestling and Boxing.

The Marine Corps recognize this fact, and are giving more complete combat conditioning to their members than ever before. But before America's program of physical training can be complete, every able man should give himself the training that helps to build a strong body and the ability to defend one's self in physical combat.

(Signed) MAJOR R. E. (DICK) HANLEY

United States Marine Corps Reserve
Officer-in-Charge, Combat Conditioning

**Major R. E. Hanley Reviewing Combat
Conditioning Practice**

BOOK'S PURPOSE

In instructing the science of self-defense to various groups of Marines, it was discovered that there was a pressing need for some sort of basic reference guide for students to use as a "memory refresher" between classes. This book is the answer.

Since it was first printed as a pocket reference guide for Marine students of Jiu Jitsu Defense there have been innumerable requests for a second edition available to the general public. And because today as never before the knowledge of self-defense in physical combat is a necessary part of every man's makeup, these requests have been granted.

With more and more men being called into Uncle Sam's Armed Forces daily, the burden of protecting the home folks is doubly great for those of us left behind. For this reason, every able man owes it to America's loved ones to equip himself with the ability to give protection when the unforseen emergency arrives. Careful study of the methods described on the pages to follow will provide YOU with that ability.

Remember one thing—this book was not written to teach you a group of "tricks" to amuse your friends. Because only serious injury, or even death, can result from the forceful application of many of the holds it illustrates and teaches. In other words, this book was created only to help men when they're "fighting for keeps."

CONTENTS

Page

Statement by Major Hanley....................2
Picture Major Hanley........................3
Book's Purpose..............................4
Contents 5
Preparing for Jiu Jitsu Falls.................6
Jiu Jitsu Defense Falling Exercises...........7-9
Edge of Hand Slash..........................10-11
Wrist Throw.................................12-13
Kick Defense Against Club and Knife..........14
Front Hip Throw..............................15
Back Hip Throw...............................16
Over Shoulder Throw..........................17
Circle Throw................................18-19
Straight Foot Throw.........................20-21
Break for Front Hug.........................22-23
Break for Back Hug Under Arms...............24-25
Defense for Back Hold Over Arms..............27
Kidney Blow Against Boxer....................28
Shoulder Pressure Arm Break..................29
Break Against Elbow.........................30-31
Lean Back Arm Break.........................32-33
Arm Hold for Marching Prisoner..............34-35
Slash at Throat with Kick Back...............36
Crossed Arm Choke When Knocked Down..........37
Choke Breaks................................38-39
Break for Straight Arm Choke................40-41
Wrap Around Choke............................42
Strangle Hold with Knee in Back..............43
Defense Against Knife When Knocked Down.....44-45
Arm Lever Back Strangle......................46
Crab Claw Throw..............................47
Defense Against Knife Jab from Side..........48
Cross Arm Choke..............................48
Bent Arm Hold................................49
Dangerous Back Push..........................50
Club or Stick Defense.......................51-64
Disarming 65-71
Defense Against Machete, Club, Knife........72-73
Disarming a Third Party......................74
Safe Method of Searching Your Prisoner.......74
Bayonet Disarming 75-82
Defense Against Bayonet......................83
Fox Hole Trick...............................84
First Aid 85-91
Combat Conditioning Program.................92-95

PREPARING FOR JIU JITSU DEFENSE FALLS AND THROWS

It is important to prepare the body for Jiu Jitsu slams.

After a little practice you will be able to throw and be thrown practically from any position without shock or injury to the body.

It is very important to exercise as shown on pages 3, 4 and 5.

This will give you an idea on how to prepare for falls. Be sure to relax. When throwing an opponent in practice, grasp his sleeve near the muscle and hold him back slightly. Use either hand.

JIU JITSU DEFENSE FALLING EXERCISE

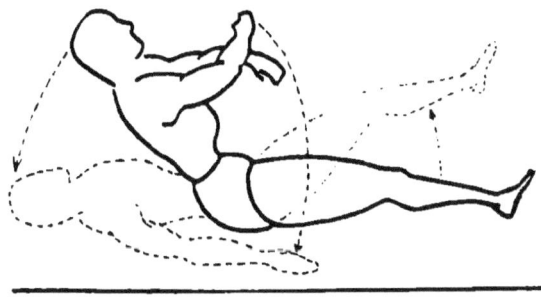

JIU JITSU FALLING EXERCISES

1. Lay flat, feet stretched out, chin pulled in, cross extended arms across chest and let them fall on mat in a slapping position, about 45° from body. Cup hands slightly. Repeat this many times.

2. Sit up, cross arms and fall back. Hand should slap mat at same time back does.

3. (Not sketched.) Lay flat on mat, cross arms. Rotate body to the left. The left arm then slaps the mat 45° from body. The right leg swings across the left leg, slapping the mat with the sole of the foot. Same movement for the right. Repeat this many times.

JIU JITSU DEFENSE FALLING EXERCISE

FALLING EXERCISES

When you are thrown by an opponent with the hip throw or over-shoulder throw, twist your body while falling in same position as sketched. Your hand must be 45° from your body. Slap hard against mat at the moment of impact of your body.

JIU JITSU DEFENSE FALLING EXERCISE

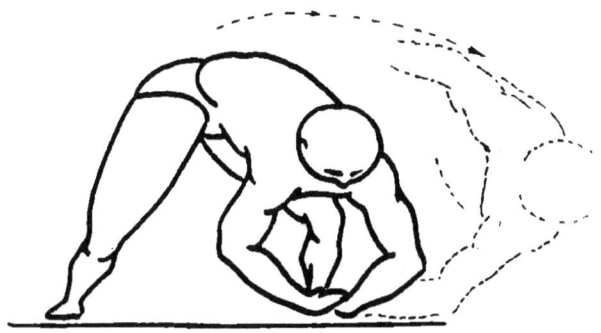

FALLING EXERCISES

In falling forward take 1 step forward. Your left foot will be extended, fingers pointing towards your body. Put your right hand on your left hand, palm down, fingers pointing toward your left hand. Your arms will then form a circle. Roll towards your left, rotating on your left arm, shoulder and back. Keep arms in a circular position. Then you will come up on your feet.

ILLUSTRATING EDGE OF HAND SLASH

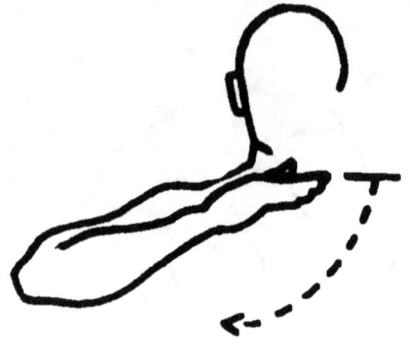

START

FINISH

EDGE OF HAND SLASH

CAUTION: These slashes are very dangerous.

Deliver slashing blow with arm slightly bent; fingers straight and close together. Palm of hand must face down. Strike either side of neck or spine close to head or to adams apple. Use either hand for slashing.

Extremely dangerous are slashes against the bridge or base of the nose.

ILLUSTRATING START AND FINISH OF WRIST THROW

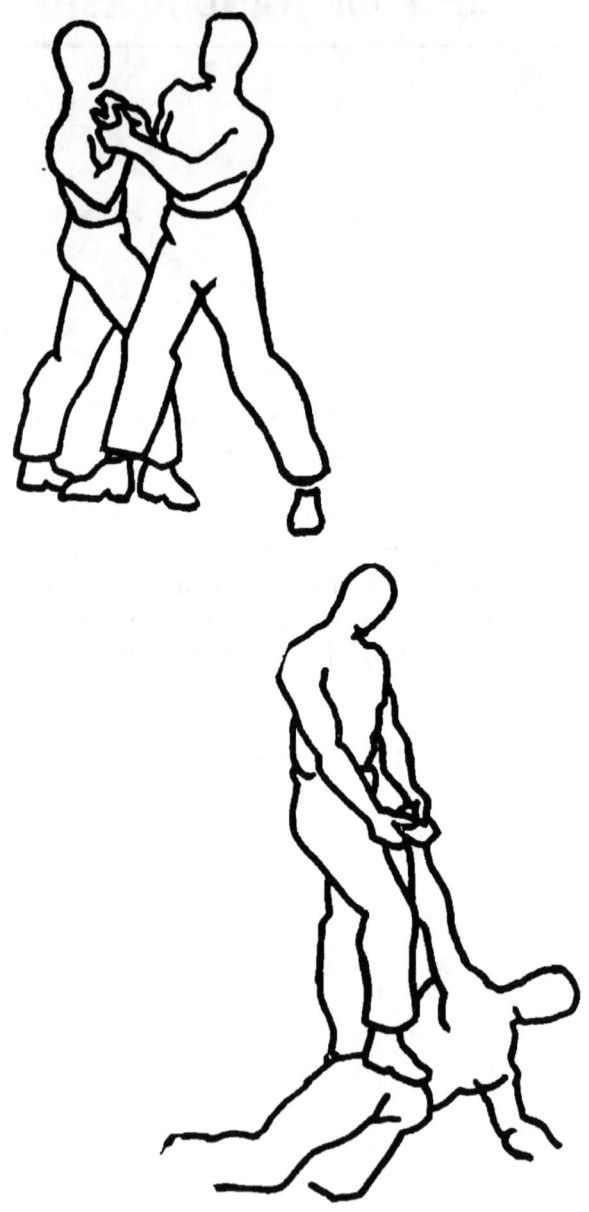

WRIST THROW

Grasp opponent's right hand with your left hand palm facing down. Your fingers are curled around his thumb. Press your thumb hard against the back of opponent's hand. Raise his hand shoulder high applying your right hand in the same manner. Twist and push to your left and force his wrist backwards and down. Place your right foot against his right foot blocking it from the back and throw him to the ground. Hold his right hand tightly and with heel of your shoe stamp into head or testicles.

KICK DEFENSE
AGAINST CLUB, KNIFE, BLOW

Pivot so as to be at right angles with the opponent. Clasp hands in front of chest to maintain balance. Kick leg straight out from hip, bringing foot back fast for additional kick. Aim at vulnerable spots, knee caps, testicles, heart, etc.

Use caution in practice.

FRONT HIP THROW

Grab your opponent's right arm at the muscle with your left hand, wrap your right arm around his waist, and turn forcing your right hip into his stomach. Lean forward to your left and pull down on his right arm—throwing him violently forward.

BACK HIP THROW

CAUTION: This fall is very dangerous. Grasp your opponent's right arm at the muscle with your left hand. Step behind him with your right foot inserting your hip against the back of his. Grasp his left arm with your right hand pulling up with your right hand and down with your left while bending your knees slightly; rotate hip upwards thus throwing him to the ground.

Finish: Hold on to his left arm tightly and while keeping him slightly off the ground kick down with the heel of your shoe into his heart or head.

OVER SHOULDER THROW

If opponent attempts to choke you from behind with his right arm around your neck, step forward slightly with your right foot and at the same time grasp his arm at the elbow with your left hand. Reach up with your right hand grasping his clothes at his right shoulder. Stoop forward suddenly, and by forcing your hips violently into his stomach, pull him over your shoulder.

CIRCLE THROW
(START)

Grasp opponent by the collar or back of arms. Force him backwards slightly. He will then push against you forcing you backwards. You will then lean back while kicking him in the stomach with either foot and pulling him towards your face. While lying flat on your back, with bent foot kick hard straight up throwing your opponent over your head.

CIRCLE THROW
(FINISH)

The author is here demonstrating how to break a fall when thrown by "Circle Throw."

The fist comes down first and you roll on your arm rolling across your shoulders and slapping the mat hard just before your back lands.

STRAIGHT FOOT THROW

Enemy is choking you from the front.

Grab his right arm at the muscle with your left hand, thumb up and with your right hand grab his coat lapel. Step back until your left foot is back, his right foot will be forward. Put your weight on your left foot. Extend your right foot to the outside of his right ankle. Trip him with your right foot by pulling and leaning towards your left and push him backwards with your right hand. This will cause him to fall on his back.

ILLUSTRATING FINISH OF STRAIGHT FOOT THROW

ILLUSTRATING BREAK FOR FRONT HUG

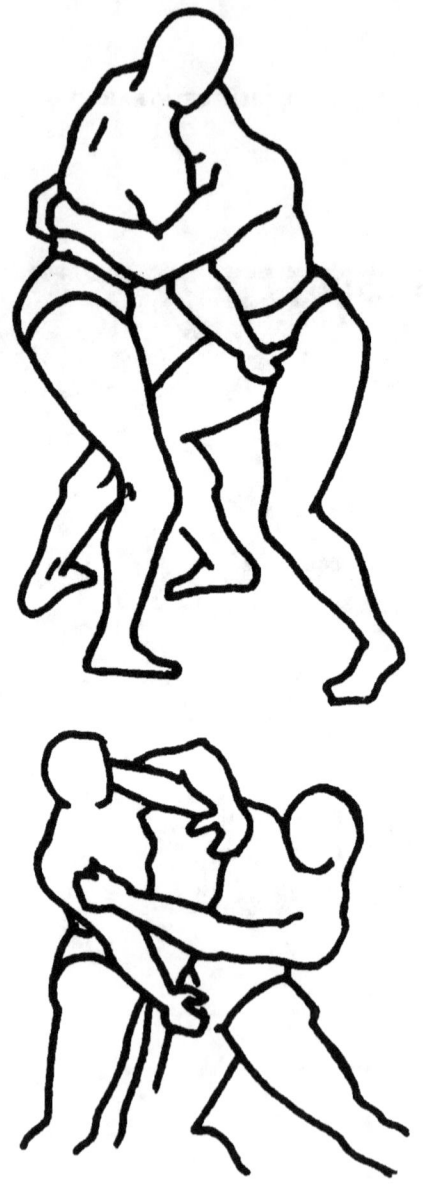

BREAK FOR FRONT HUG

1. Attempt to bite his ear. This will cause him to bend forward when you will immediately grab his testicles with your right hand which will force him to step back.

2. And with your left hand reach up and over in a circular movement forcing his right arm against your neck and shoulder. Push down hard on his arm thus causing considerable pain or break.

3. When he lowers his head use slash with your right hand against the back of his neck.

4. Or: Kick with knee into testicles.

ILLUSTRATING BREAK FOR BACK HUG UNDER ARMS

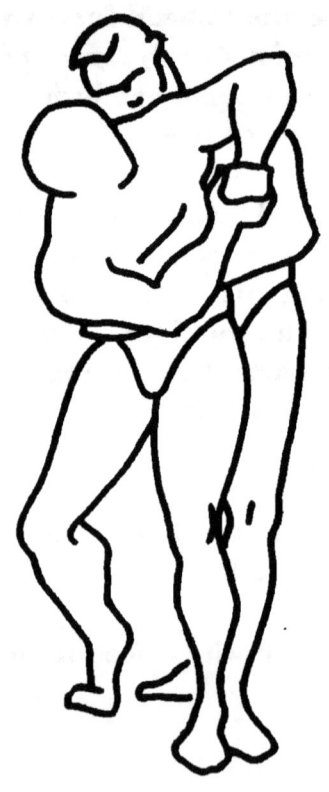

BREAK FOR BACK HUG UNDER THE ARMS

Opponent grasps you from around the waist in the back holding you tightly. Step forward with either foot and bend forward slightly. Clasp your hands shoulder high; swing hard to either side striking his head with your elbows.

Or:

Grind heel of your shoe into his toes or instep or reach back and grasp his testicles.

ILLUSTRATING DEFENSE FOR BACK HOLDS OVER ARMS

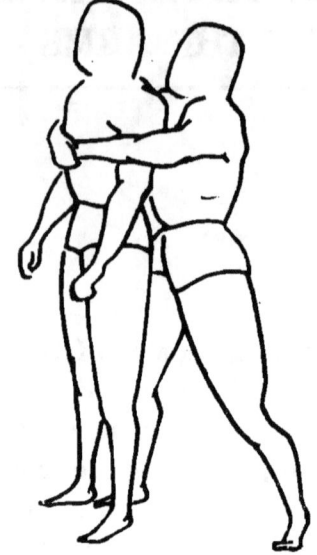

START

FINISH

DEFENSE FOR BACK HOLD OVER ARMS

If enemy grabs you from the back locking your arms against your body step forward slightly with your right foot. Clasp your hands together and at the same time taking a deep breath, bring your hands up quickly and exhaling at the same time. Then with his hands loosened, grasp his right muscle with your left hand and with your right hand grasp him high near the collar and go into the "Over Shoulder Throw"

Or:

Jab your left elbow into his kidneys.

KIDNEY BLOW AGAINST BOXER

Opponent is aiming a blow at your head with his right fist.
Side step to the left pushing his right elbow to his left with your left hand. Pivot to your right until your body is facing the same direction as his, and smash your left elbow into his ribs, kidneys, heart or testicles.

SHOULDER PRESSURE ARM BREAK

If opponent slides his right hand under your left arm pit capture it and break it by twisting your left arm around the outside of his while your right arm rests on his shoulder. Grasp your own right arm with your left hand and pull up with your left hand and lean back slightly. This will cause considerable pain or break his arm. This hold can be applied with either hand.

ILLUSTRATING BREAK AGAINST ELBOW

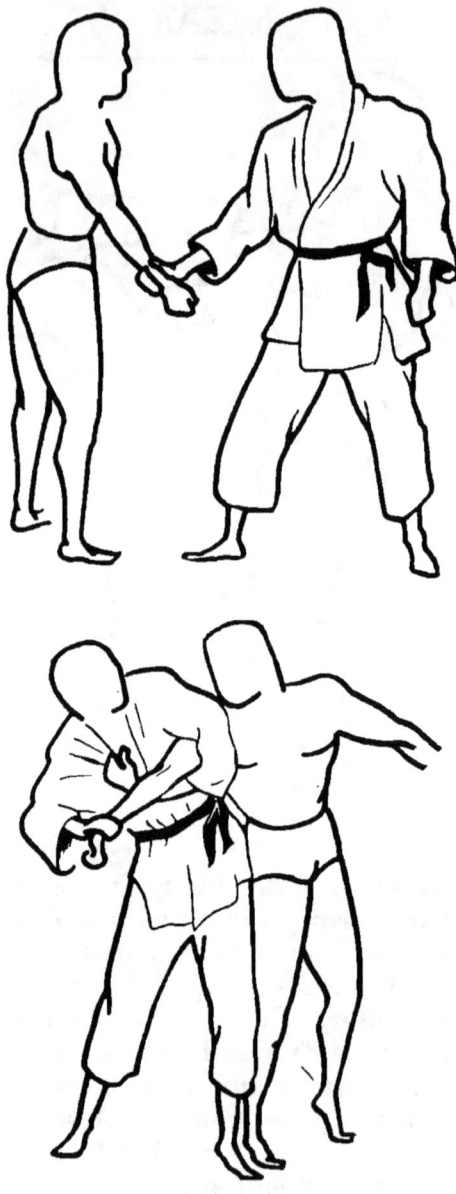

BREAK AGAINST ELBOW

Enemy attempts to strike you with his right hand, grasp his right hand with your right hand. With your thumb up, pull him toward you slightly; his arm must be rotated palm up and at same time step behind him toward your left. You will then be facing the same way. Wrap your left arm around his right arm muscle tightly and grab your own coat lapel to your right. Push your hip into his and force his captured arm down with your right hand, thereby causing considerable pain or breaking the arm.

ILLUSTRATING LEAN BACK ARM BREAK

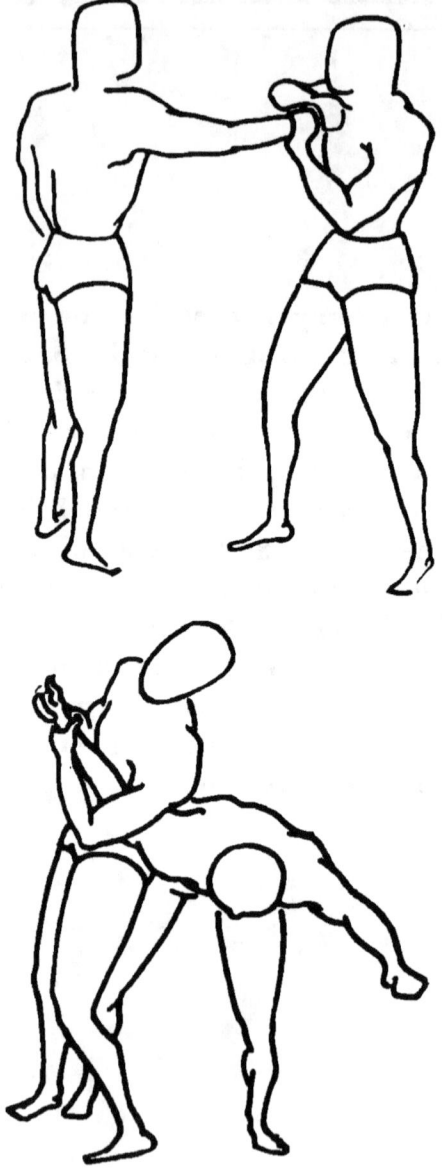

LEAN BACK ARM BREAK

Opponent grasps your collar, your shoulder or neck on your left with his right hand. Place your right hand across his hand holding it firmly in position against your body, rotate on your left foot, towards your right, so that your body is facing the same way as his. Keep his arm extended, raise your left arm, over his captured arm and clamp the elbow tight against your body anchoring his arm, his palm should be rotated up to his left, lean back in a falling position. This will break his arm very easily if he resists.

Either hand can be used. Use caution in practice.

ILLUSTRATING ARM-HOLD FOR MARCHING A PRISONER

ARM-HOLD FOR MARCHING A PRISONER

You are facing in the same direction as your opponent standing at his left. Insert your right arm between his left arm and left side. And with your left hand raise his left hand towards your shoulder —his palm facing backwards. Apply downward pressure against the back of his hand.

SLASH AT THROAT WITH KICK BACK

When attacked by enemy with a knife in his right hand, step to his left, slash your left hand into his windpipe. Grab his left hand at same time insert your left foot behind his left foot. Pull toward your right on his arm. Push back hard on his neck, causing him to take a very violent back fall. Kick into his heart, when he is down on ground. Either hand may be used. Very dangerous. Caution in practice.

CROSSED ARM CHOKE WHEN KNOCKED DOWN

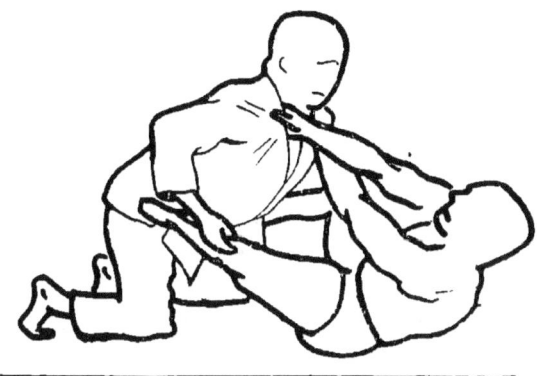

When you are knocked backwards or you miss a circle throw use a cross arm choke and push your feet into your opponent's stomach, raising your opponent slightly from the mat. This will force his neck hard into your crossed arms. Pull and twist hard on your arms and this will c a u s e immediate strangulation. To counter this choke, slash your extended fingers and hand into his exposed throat or grab for his testicles.

This is very dangerous in practice. Use caution.

ILLUSTRATING CHOKE BREAKS

CHOKE BREAKS

Clasp your hands forming a V. Thrust up hard against the arms and strike face with a downward movement; in so doing opponent's nose and face is smashed.

Alternative Action:

Clasp your hands forming a V. Thrust up hard against the arms thus breaking the choke hold. Grasp him by the shoulders pulling him toward you. Then drive your knee into his testicles.

No. 2

Enemy attempts to choke you:

Jab hand with fingers held rigid hard into opponent's windpipe. Either hand may be used. Take one step forward and thrust knee into testicles.

ILLUSTRATING BREAK FOR STRAIGHT ARM CHOKE

START

FINISH

BREAK FOR STRAIGHT ARM CHOKE

Enemy grasps your throat with both hands:

Throw right arm over opponent's arms grasping his right wrist. Step back slightly with right foot. Thrust up your left hand against opponent's right elbow keeping a firm grip on his right wrist with your right hand. Pull him forward slightly with right hand and bear down on his right elbow with left, breaking choke. Follow through with slash against arm or back of neck.

WRAP AROUND CHOKE

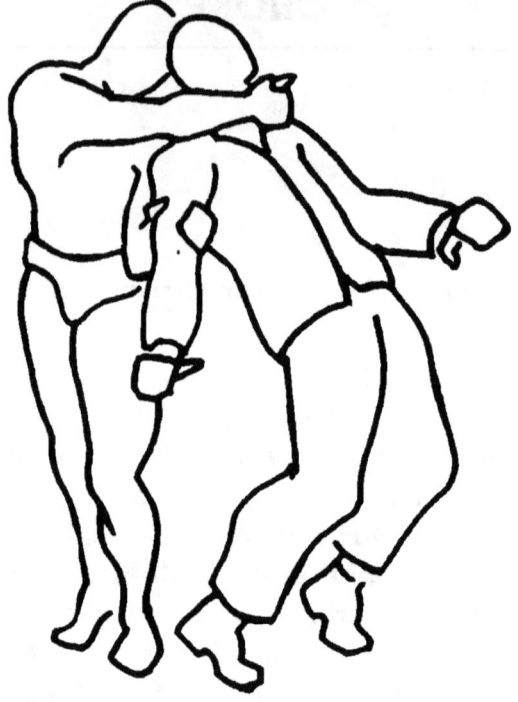

With your opponent directly in front of you reach out with right hand and grasp collar behind left ear — thumb down. Grab right arm back of muscle and pull him violently toward you and at the same time stepping directly behind him. Keep tight grasp of collar and your right forearm stiff against his windpipe. Then bend him back and insert your left arm between his back and left arm. Force your knuckles into his back and pull back hard with your right arm—strangling him.

STRANGLE HOLD WITH KNEE IN BACK

Step behind opponent and clasp your right forearm against his windpipe pulling his head back slightly. Your left arm is extended over his left shoulder —grasp your left muscle with your right hand and push against the back of his head with the palm of your left hand. Insert your right knee into his back and bring him back slowly, strangling him.

ILLUSTRATING DEFENSE AGAINST KNIFE WHEN KNOCKED DOWN

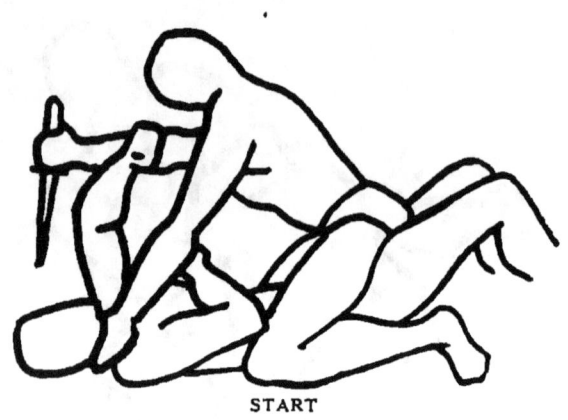

START

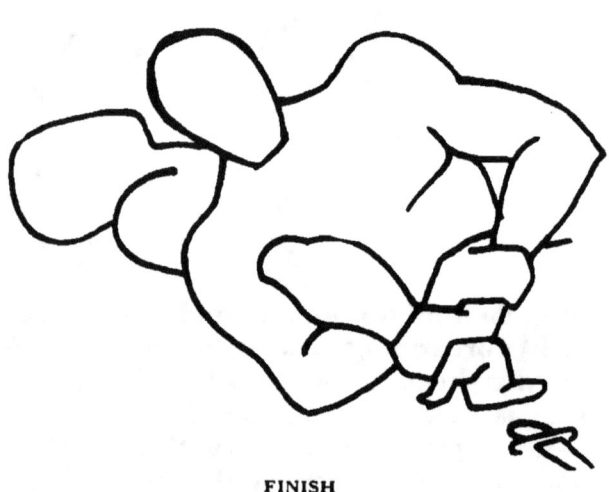

FINISH

DEFENSE AGAINST KNIFE WHEN KNOCKED DOWN

You are knocked flat on your back —

Enemy is holding you down with his left hand and with his right hand he is attempting to stab you. Slash your left hand against his arm at the same time grasping his wrist. Throw him to your left by raising your right leg and hip, hold on to his right wrist and wrap your right arm over his right arm. Apply pressure by clasping your left wrist with your thumb down.

ARM LEVER BACK STRANGLE

Enemy attacks you with knife in his right hand:

Seize his right wrist with your right hand with your thumb to the left. Turn so that you are behind enemy. Extend your left leg behind him—wrap your left arm around his neck from the front forcing his head back at the same time pulling this right arm across your chest—thereby strangling him.

CRAB CLAW THROW

This is used for disarming against a knife:

The action is done by grasping his right wrist with your left hand and resting your right on the ground and jumping against his body with your feet spread apart; your left foot high against his waist and your right against the back of the ankles. Twist towards the left causing your opponent to take a very vicious fall.

DEFENSE AGAINST KNIFE JAB FROM THE SIDE

Enemy has knife in his right hand and aims it from the side towards your stomach:

Slash your left hand against the inside of his wrist blocking the swing. Force his arm to the side and back. Step in with your right foot and wrap your right arm over his right arm while forcing his arm up and back with your left hand. This will cause him to drop the knife. This will automatically cause him to bend forward, then slash with your right hand against the back of his neck knocking him unconscious.

NOT ILLUSTRATED

CROSS ARM CHOKE

Choking enemy when you knock him down flat on his back:

Sit on his chest! Grasp his collar in back of his ears with your hands crossed, your thumbs are on the outside of his collar. Keep him flat on the ground by forcing either forearm into his windpipe. Lean hard on your arm while holding tightly to his collar and slip your other hand under his head and grasp your anchored hand and pull. This will cause immediate strangulation.

TO COUNTER THIS CHOKE: Jab your fingers hard into his windpipe.

BENT ARM HOLD

Opponent attempts to attack you: Grasp his wrist with your left hand shoulder high. Step in with your right foot and force your right arm under his shoulder; grasping the top of your left hand and applying downward pressure on the wrist while pushing up with your shoulder. Keep a firm grip! Now kick with your right foot against his right heel to disarm him while knocking him down.

Now jump on his body with both feet—heels first.

DANGEROUS "BACK PUSH"

When enemy dashes directly at you, take one step to your left side. Face him. Bend down suddenly and insert your right arm between his legs and grab his belt from the back and pull hard. At the same time straighten up and slash your left hand into his throat or face.

Or:

Push hard on his chest forcing him to fall on his back.

Jump on him with the heels of your shoes first.

NOT ILLUSTRATED

CLUB OR STICK DEFENSE

A short club or stick, about 18 inches long can be used as a very effective weapon. It should be held in either hand alongside your forearm with the end of club or stick protruding about three inches. In this manner it can be used to slash against an enemy's throat, arms, kidneys, back of the neck, against the nose, against knife slashes, punches, kicks across the shins. A quick way to eliminate enemy is to jab the stick into the pit of the stomach, throat, mouth, eyes, testicles and into the heart. Use caution in practice.

SEE FOLLOWING ILLUSTRATIONS

ILLUSTRATING CLUB OR STICK DEFENSE FOR M. P. OR POLICE OFFICER

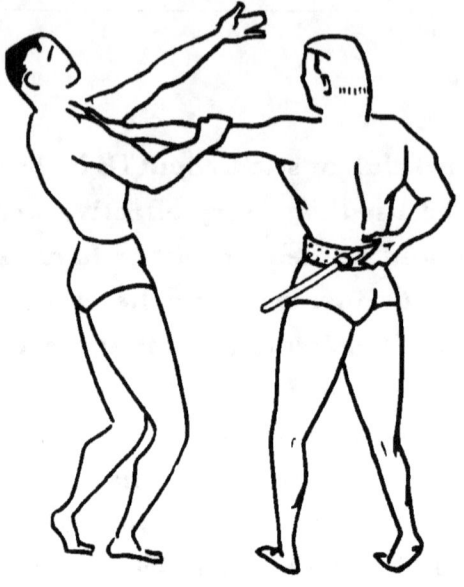

START

FINISH

CLUB OR STICK DEFENSE

FOR M. P. OR POLICE OFFICER

When enemy attempts to close in on you hold him back with your left hand and reach back with your right hand. Grasp your club as sketched. Jab hard into stomach, heart, neck, mouth, eyes, windpipe; slash against the back or side of neck, against the wrist or jab in the testicles. Use caution in practice.

TO HANDLE AN UNRULY PRISONER

Grab him at the back of his collar, so that that you are directly behind him. Hold your club in the middle with your right hand. Force your club and hand between his legs so that your fingers are pointing up. Pull hard up on your club and push him forward slightly with your left hand, which is still holding his collar tightly. By pulling steadily on your club you will then force him to march forward.

CLUB OR STICK DEFENSE

Clasp club or stick with both hands, thumbs up and strike your opponent in neck. Follow up by kicking your knee into testicles. Very effective is blow across the bridge of the nose. It will kill a man instantly.

CLUB OR STICK DEFENSE

Official U. S. Navy Photograph

Illustration shows proper method of defense against knife slash. Club or stick can be used as a weapon against knife slash. Drive club hard against hand holding knife. This will disarm him.

CLUB OR STICK DEFENSE
START

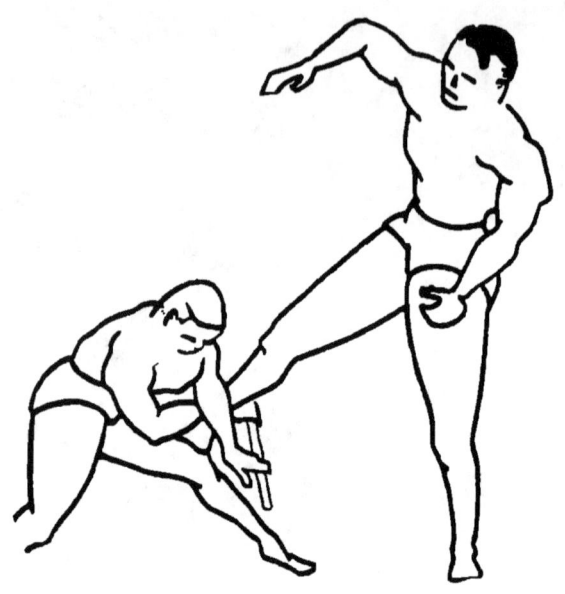

If enemy attempts to kick you, cross your right hand under your left hand while holding the club in your right hand. Bring it under his leg and grasp club with your crossed left hand, pull up.

CLUB OR STICK DEFENSE
FINISH

Lean back slightly, applying a lot of pressure with the stick against the shins, twist suddenly either way, forcing your opponent to face away from you. Hold tight on stick and kick up hard with your right foot into stomach or testicles. Use caution in practice.

CLUB OR STICK DEFENSE

Official U. S. Navy Photograph

Illustration shows stick or club defense against kick.

CLUB OR STICK DEFENSE

Official U. S. Navy Photograph

Illustration shows proper method of silencing a sentry. Complete description on next pages.

CLUB OR STICK DEFENSE
START

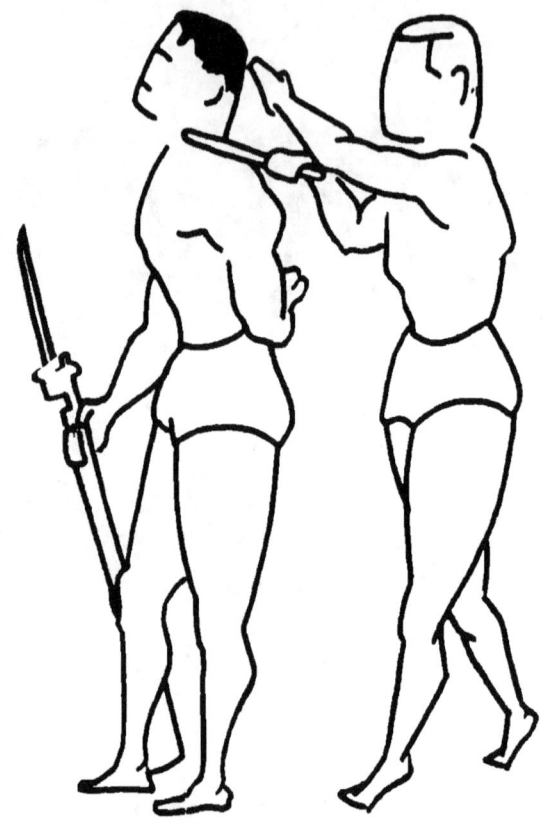

Silencing and disarming a sentry. Approach silently then quickly cross your left hand over your right hand which is holding the club. Force the club around his throat. Grasp it quickly with your left hand. Force it against his windpipe crushing it. VERY dangerous in practice.

CLUB OR STICK DEFENSE
FINISH

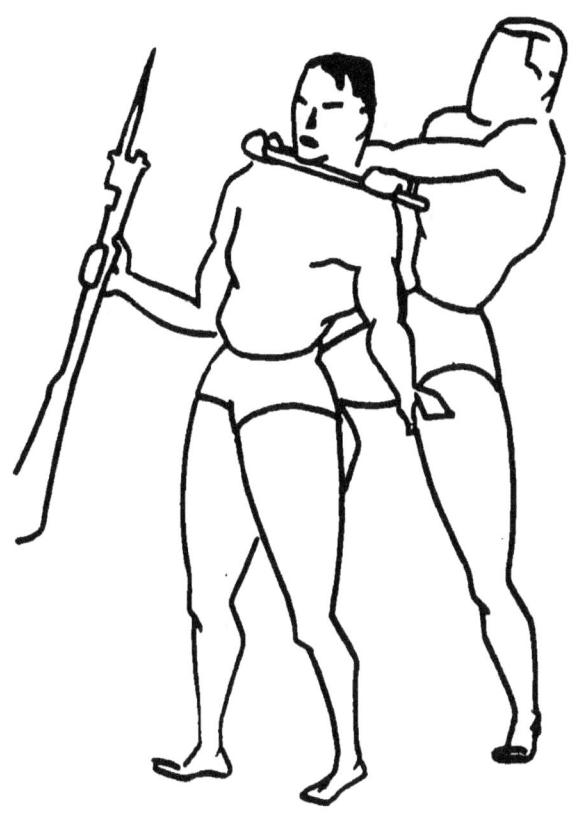

Pull back on club, push knee into his back violently breaking his spine. Force body to ground slowly, holding tightly to stick which will strangle him. Very dangerous in practice. Use caution.

CLUB OR STICK DEFENSE
START

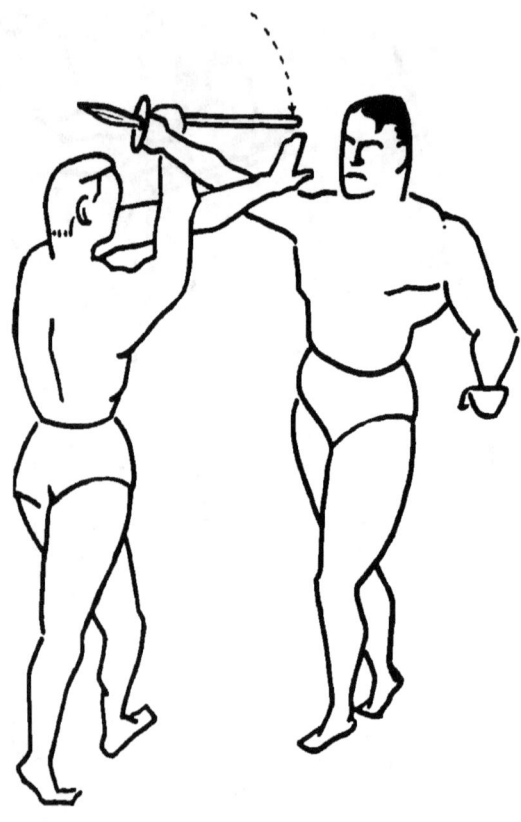

Enemy jabs knife down at you. Cross your right hand over your left, while holding your club with your right hand. Receive the knife jab between your crossed hands. Force the club over his forearm towards your crossed left hand. Grab it.

CLUB OR STICK DEFENSE
FINISH

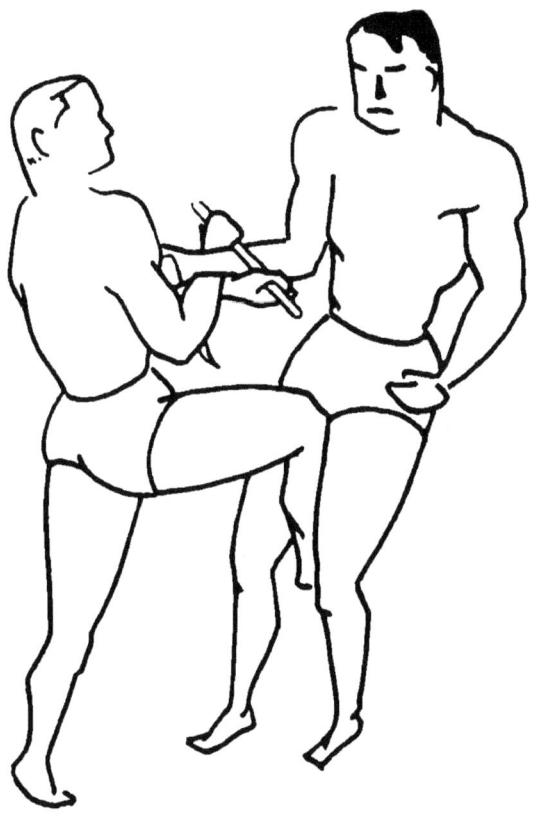

Force down on club which will bend him forward. Step into him and kick hard with your knee into his testicles. At the same time pressing down on his forearm which will break it. Use caution in practice.

CLUB OR STICK DEFENSE

Official U. S. Navy Photograph

Illustration shows proper method of blocking downward knife slash.

DISARMING

The following pages will consist of proper methods of disarming an enemy armed with the following weapons:

PISTOL
RIFLE AND BAYONET
MACHETE
KNIFE
CLUB

All of disarming action is very violent and dangerous. Use caution in practice.

ILLUSTRATING DISARMING TRICK NO. 1

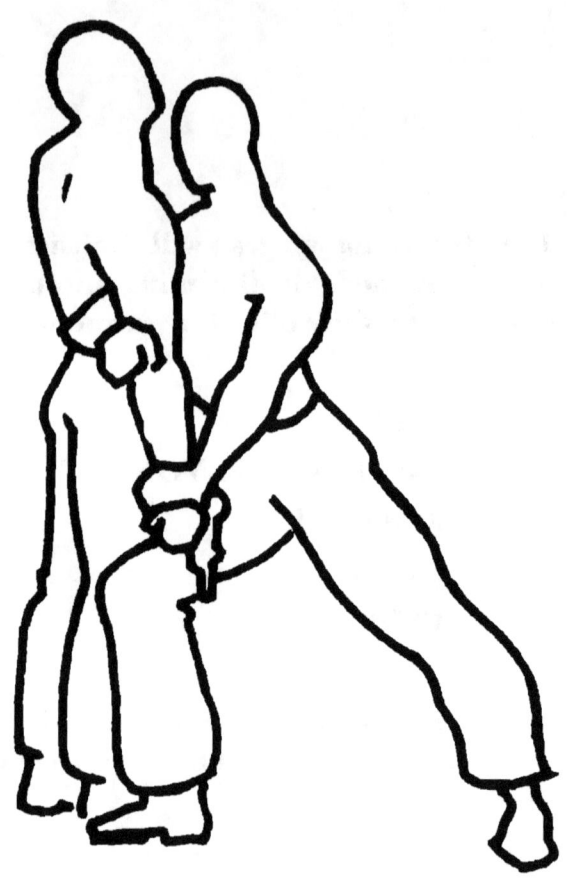

DISARMING TRICK No. 1

Your enemy attempts to use weapon from the side:

Grasp his right wrist with your left hand. Step forward with right foot while sliding your right arm between his arm and side. Crook arm forming an "L" clenching fist tightly. Strike back of elbow sharply with center of your forearm. This will cause him considerable pain forcing him to drop his weapon.

If he attempts to throw his free hand about your neck, go into "Over Shoulder Throw."

ILLUSTRATING DISARMING TRICK NO. 2

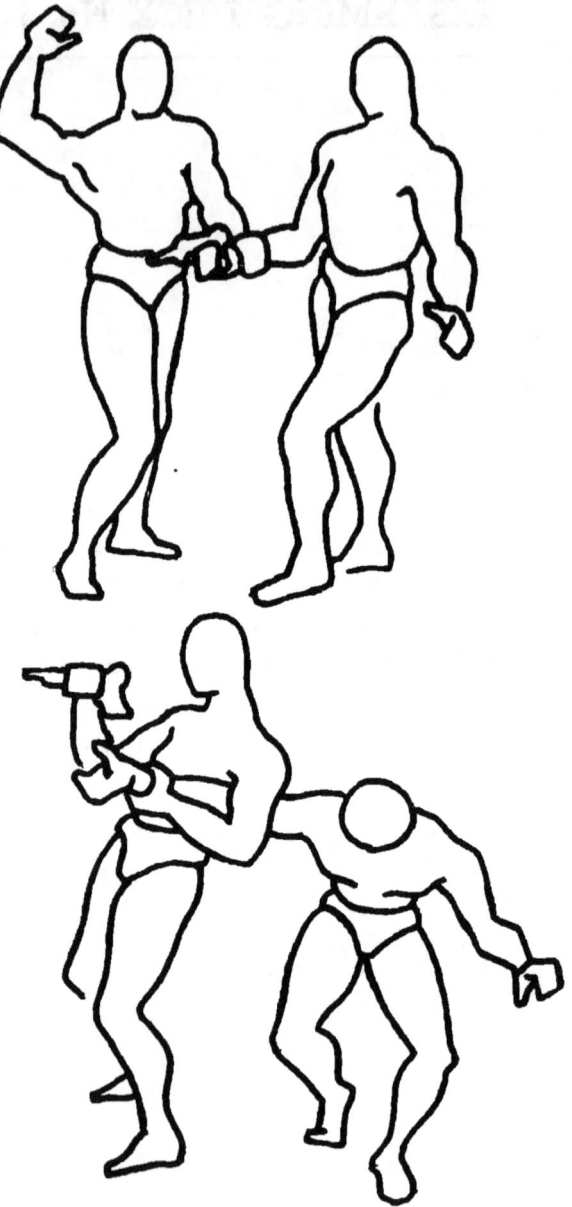

DISARMING TRICK No. 2

Your enemy attempts to capture you and holds weapon to your stomach:

Clasp his right hand at the wrist with your left hand (your thumb facing down). At the same time step back with your right foot—180 degrees; holding his arm and pulling slightly while rotating and twisting it palm up towards your body. Lean back and down against his arm clamping your elbow against his arm and holding it tightly to your side.

Disarm by turning gun toward his face with your right hand. Strike him with captured weapon on the back of his neck. Continue holding him by leaning back against his arm.

ILLUSTRATING DISARMING TRICK NO. 3

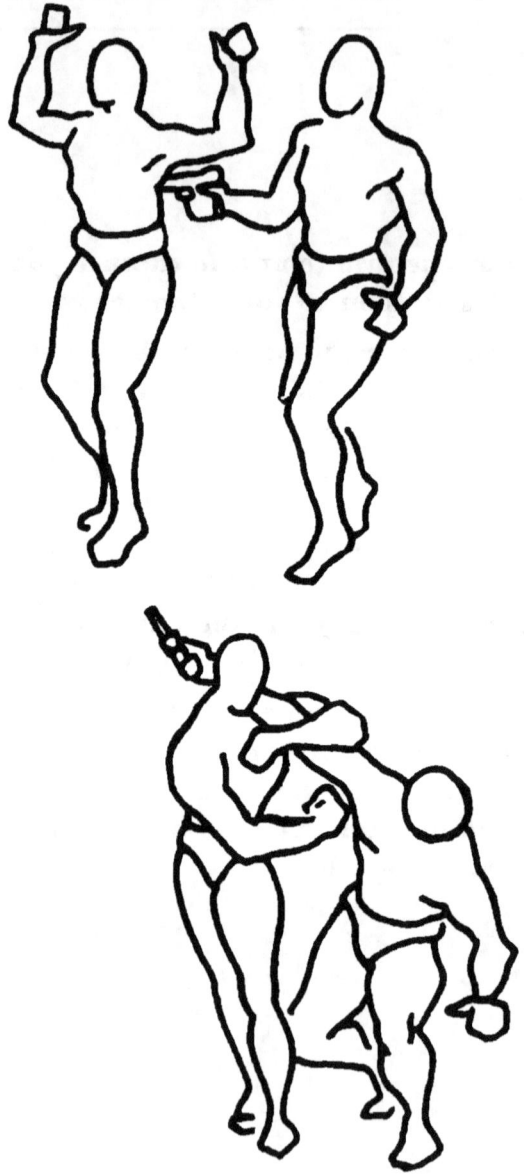

DISARMING TRICK No. 3

Your enemy attempts to capture you; marching you with weapon in your side. He is one step behind you:

Stop suddenly with right foot forward; sweeping your left hand down along your side and back over his arm in a rotating motion anchoring his hand against your shoulder and neck. Press down hard against his elbow and strike his face with free hand or knee.

Or:

Reach back over your head with your right hand and disarm him. Then hit him in back of neck with weapon.

ILLUSTRATING DEFENSE AGAINST MACHETE - CLUB - KNIFE

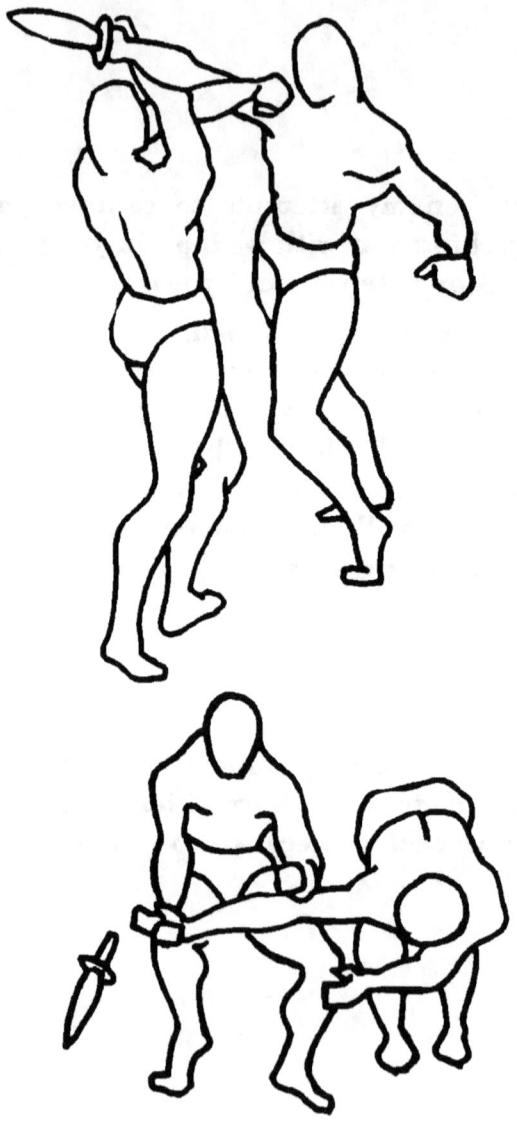

DEFENSE AGAINST MACHETE - CLUB - KNIFE

Your enemy attempts to strike you across head and shoulders with weapon with his right hand:

Cross hands above your head, right hand in front of left. Receive the blow in the "V" formed by hands. Then grasp his wrist with your right hand rotating his arm towards you so that his hand will face up. At the same time slide your right foot back about 50 degrees. Apply pressure downward on his elbow with your left forearm.

To put enemy out of action force him slowly to ground holding him firmly. Step over his right arm with your left foot and sit on his shoulder and break his arm by pulling up hard.

DISARMING A THIRD PARTY

You suddenly come upon an enemy holding up one of your own men at the point of a pistol. Step up quietly with your right foot extended and bring your right hand up against his wrist with your thumb up and your left hand simultaneously coming down on his forearm with the palm down. Bend his forearm up and backwards against the shoulder, and at the same time step behind him with your right leg tripping and disarming him. Now, with your enemy lying on the ground jump on him, driving your heels into his body.

SAFE METHOD OF SEARCHING YOUR PRISONER

Walk enemy against a wall or tree with his hands upraised. Force him to keep his hands in the same spot. Make him walk backwards until he stands on his tiptoe with his feet spread apart, which will cause him to lean against the wall.

Hold your pistol at a safe distance out of his reach. You can then search him taking care that your foot is next to his foot.

If he attempts to resist you can trip him by sweeping his legs from under him which will cause him to fall flat on his face.

BAYONET DISARMING

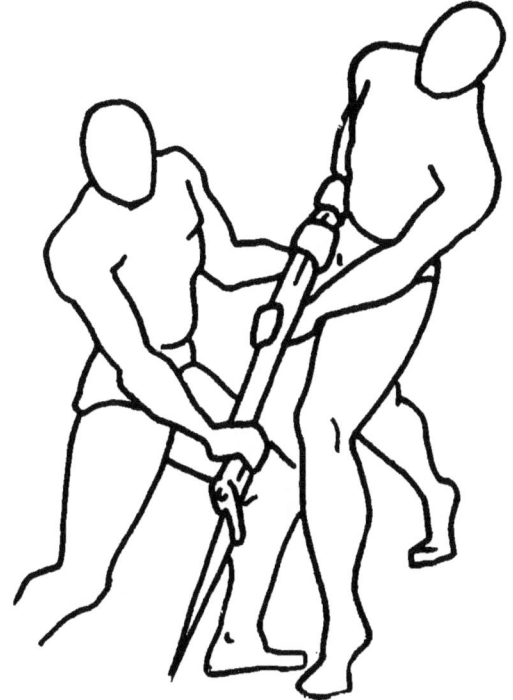

You are being attacked by enemy armed with bayonet; He is aiming for your body.

Bring your right foot behind you and grasp the muzzle of his rifle with your right hand palm down—your left hand grasps the balance of his rifle palm up. Push up with your left hand and down with your right hand—pushing bayonet into ground. Keep your right foot to the left of bayonet by stepping directly behind him. Pushing him forward violently. This will force him to let go of rifle. You will then be able to attack him with his own rifle.

BAYONET DISARMING

Official U. S. Navy Photograph

Illustration shows bayonet disarming by forcing bayonet in the ground.

RIFLE AND BAYONET DISARMING

Official U. S. Navy Photograph

Action No. 1.

Enemy attacks you and is pointing bayonet at your body.

RIFLE AND BAYONET DISARMING

Official U. S. Navy Photograph

Action No. 2.

Step or pivot towards your left, grasp rifle in back of the bayonet with your left hand, pulling up and with your right hand grasp the back of the balance of rifle, pulling down.

RIFLE AND BAYONET DISARMING

Official U. S. Navy Photograph

Action No. 3.

Take one step back which will force his arm and rifle to point backwards and downwards.

RIFLE AND BAYONET DISARMING

Official U. S. Navy Photograph

Action No. 4—Finish.

Your enemy's forward momentum will force him to let go of rifle. Reverse the same and slash at the back of neck. Use caution in practice.

RIFLE AND BAYONET DISARMING

START

Official U. S. Navy Photograph

At close quarters enemy attempts to drive rifle, held flat, directly in front of him into your face. Cross arms and twist to your left.

RIFLE AND BAYONET DISARMING

Official U. S. Navy Photograph

By twisting to your left it will cause him to let go of the rifle. Now reverse rifle and bayonet and attack him. Use caution in practice.

DEFENSE AGAINST BAYONET

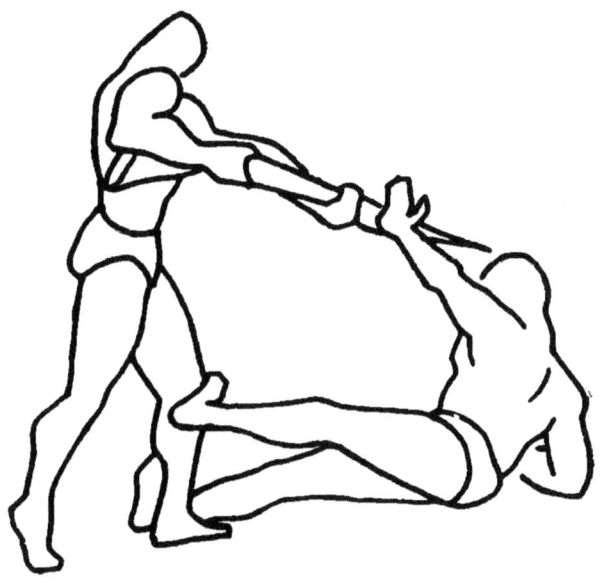

If knocked to ground and attacked, hook right foot about your enemy's ankle, toe in. Pull towards you and push with other foot against inside of knee joint. Parry bayonet thrust and disarm.

FOX-HOLE TRICK

Coming out of foxhole, clasp enemy's leading foot, using hand on same side. Thrust hard with forearm against inside of knee joint, pushing out and back. Climb across enemy using knee in testicles and choke.

This may be performed with either hand.

FIRST AID

1. Prompt emergency treatment given an injured person while awaiting regular medical attendance is called FIRST AID.

2. To be able to give efficient help to wounded or direct and assist others in case of injury to himself a person must be familiar with the details of first aid.

3. When not certain what first aid is to be given, you must leave injured person alone, send for medical assistance, but must protect him from exposure, further injury and inexperienced efforts of others.

4. When certain of what is to be done, administer first aid and then send for medical assistance.

5. Keep cool, act quickly, be gentle and do not attempt to do too much while administering first aid.

6. To avoid injury to yourself and others you must be well drilled in the performance of duties, be familiar with hazards involved and be careful.

7. Carelessness and ignorance are two things most responsible for injuries, both of which are avoidable.

TREATMENT OF WOUNDS

1. A wound is an injury in which the skin is pierced or broken.

2. Hemorrhage and shock are caused from severe wounds, which are very dangerous.

3. Delayed healing or blood poisoning is caused from open wounds.

4. Examine the wound; control hemorrhage; prevent infection; prevent shock or treat it if present are the four steps in administration of first aid.

5. To examine and treat a wound, unbutton, unlace or rip or cut off clothing, shoes, leggings or boots.

6. The wound should never be touched with the fingers, clothing or other unsterilized objects.

CONTROL OF HEMORRHAGE

1. Bleeding is the common name for hemorrhage.
2. Arterial, venous and capillary are the three varieties of hemorrhages.
3. Blood from an arterial hemorrhage comes out in heavy spurts with each heart beat and is bright red.
4. Blood from a venous hemorrhage comes out in a slow steady stream and is dark red or purple.
5. Blood from a capillary hemorrhage oozes out of a cut surface.
6. Arterial hemorrhage is the most dangerous of all three.
7. Natural and artificial means are used to control hemorrhage.
8. To stop a hemorrhage you must form a clot in the blood vessel or wound.
9. Capillary hemorrhage is usually controlled naturally.
10. Pressure of the fingers, elevation, use of tourniquet and pressure on bleeding point are four artificial means of hemorrhage control.
11. To stop an arterial hemorrhage you must exert pressure on the blood vessel with the fingers on the side toward the heart.
12. An arterial hemorrhage in the scalp should be controlled by the pressure of thumbs or fingers in front of the ear just above the place where the lower jaw can be felt working in the socket.
13. An arterial hemorrhage in the neck and head should be controlled by the pressure of thumbs or fingers deep into the neck in front of the strongly marked muscle which reaches from behind the ear to the upper part of the breast bone.
14. An arterial hemorrhage in the shoulder and armpits should be controlled by the pressure of thumbs or fingers outward against the bone just behind the inner border of the large muscle of the arm.
15. An arterial hemorrhage in the thigh, leg or foot should be controlled by the pressure of thumbs or fingers at the upper part of the inside of the thigh where the large artery passes over the bone.

16. The part of the body which is bleeding is elevated to control a hemorrhage.
17. Elevation of the body is usually effective when it is a capillary hemorrhage of the limbs and slight venous or arterial hemorrhage of the hands, legs or feet.
18. Only when other means fail should a tourniquet be employed to stop a hemorrhage.
19. In making a tourniquet the following should be done. Make a pad or compress using a cork or smooth round stone wrapped in bandage. Place pad at the proper place over the blood vessel. Tie a band (bandage, handkerchief, etc.) closely around the limb over pad. Tighten the band by passing a stick or bayonet through it and twisting it slowly until the bleeding stops. Then fix stick in place with bandage.
20. In adjusting a tourniquet you must be careful not to use too much force or be rough.
21. The following precautions should be taken in a tourniquet case. (1) Never cover over a tourniquet. (2) On an attached tag mark TOURNIQUET, also the date and hour when applied. (3) Every medical man with whom the patient comes in contact with must be told that he is wearing a tourniquet. (4) The tourniquet must be loosened every half hour or the limb may die. It can be tightened again if bleeding occurs.
22. When other methods fail or injury is so located as not to permit pressure on the artery, then only should pressure be applied on the bleeding point to control a hemorrhage.
23. Pressure is exterted by pressing a sterile pad in the wound and fixing it firmly in position.

WOUND DRESSING

1. Iodine should be generously applied to a wound with applicator before applying a dressing, except in the case of a missile penetrating the muscles or soft part of the body.
2. When a missile has entered or passed through the muscle or soft parts, protect it with contents of first-aid packet without attempting to clean it.
3. To apply the dressing, carefully remove the paper without unfolding the compressor bandage and grasp the outside folds of the bandage between the thumb and forefingers. Open the

compress by pulling on the two rolls, holding one in each hand; apply the compress to the wound; then wrap the bandage around limb or part and tie the ends together or fasten them with safety pins. Be sure not to touch the inside of the compress with anything.

4. To apply dressing on two opposite wounds, open compress without unrolling the bandage, over one wound; another opened compress over the other wound, holding both dressings in place with the bandage of the latter.

5. If compress is too small to cover the wound, find and break the stitch holding the compress together and unfold it. Use several compresses if necessary. The unpapered side of the compress is placed next the wound.

SHOCK

1. Shock is a sudden vital depression due to injury or emotion which makes an untoward impression upon the nervous system.

2. The symptoms of shock is that the face pales and becomes pinched with an anxious and frightened appearance; patient gets weak, faint and cold; skin is cold and clammy, pulse weak and rapid; breathing is sighing and irregular.

3. For the treatment of shock you must control hemorrhage; send for doctor; place patient horizontally with head low; loosen all tight clothing; avoid unnecessary movement; supply warmth.

4. First aid treatment should be given patient before moving.

5. To supply warmth, use hot-water bottles, canteens filled with hot water, warm stones or bricks or blankets and heavy clothing.

6. The heated articles should be wrapped in cloth and then placed under the armpits and between the legs.

7. In applying heated articles, you must be very careful to prevent burning or scalding.

SPRAINS

1. The straining or tearing of the ligaments and capsule which surround a joint is called a sprain.

2. A sudden twist or wrench will cause a sprain.

3. Pain, heat and swelling, followed by discoloration of the skin are symptoms of sprain.

4. The immediate treatment for sprain is to pack joint in crushed ice until it is well chilled, then apply pressure bandage. Repeat at 24 to 48 hour intervals.

5. When swelling has developed, elevate joint if possible and apply heat and cold alternately at 24 to 48 hour intervals, applying pressure bandage between treatments.

6. Absolute rest must be provided for the sprained member.

7. Splint must be used to prevent the patient from moving the joint.

8. The sprained joint must be rested for at least a few days.

DISLOCATIONS

1. A joint injury wherein the head of the bone slips out of its socket is called a dislocation.

2. Deformity, unusual appearance, seen by comparing injured joint with well side, limited movement, paint, shock and usually swelling are the symptoms of a dislocation.

3. In treating a dislocation, place injured member in position most comfortable to patient and cover joint with cold wet cloths. Send for a doctor.

4. Because of risk of injury do not attempt to replace the dislocated bone.

FRACTURES

1. A break in a bone is called a fracture.

2. When there is no wound extending from the broken bone through the skin, is called a simple fracture.

3. When a wound extends from the broken bone through the skin is a compound fracture.

4. Infection from the outside is the added danger from a compound fracture.

5. It is called a complicated fracture where damage was done to adjoining large vessels, nerves or muscles.

6. Improper handling will produce or aggravate shock.

7. All fractures should be handled very gently.

8. When a patient has a fractured thigh, pelvis or back, administer first aid and send for a doctor.

9. Signs of a fracture are pain, swelling, deformity, unnatural mobility, loss of power, usually shortening of limb and a sensation of grating when broken ends of bone move against each other.

10. In treatment of a simple fracture you straighten the limb by pulling gently but firmly on its end.

11. If the patient is able to walk or to be transported to medical assistance, a splant should be put on.

12. For a compound fracture you must treat the wounds or hemorrhage first, then apply the treatment for a simple fracture.

SPLINTS

1. The following can be used for temporary or immediate use for splints: Shingles, pieces of boards, sticks, chicken wire, bayonet scabbards, rain spout cut to fit the limb or bunch of twigs.

2. The splints should be well padded on the side to be applied next to the skin before using.

3. In securing the splints they must be securely bound by bandaging above and below the point of fracture, never over it.

4. The opposite leg of the body may be used as a splint for a fractured leg.

5. For a fracture of the forearm the following should be done: The forearm should be flexed across the body to a right angle, thumb up. The splints should be applied, one to the inner side, extending to the finger tips, the other to the outer surface, extending to the wrist.

6. For a fracture of the upper arm, the following should be done: If the lower part of the bone is broken, the splints should be applied, one in front, the other in rear. If the middle or upper part of the bone is broken, the splints should be applied, one on the inner side, the other to the outer side.

7. The forearm should be supported by a sling.
8. When the collarbone is fractured the forearm should be flexed across the front of the body, to a right angle. Forearm should be supported by a sling.
9. For a fracture of the leg or ankle, the splint should be applied on the outside and one on the inside, both extending from just below the knee to beyond the foot.
10. First-aid treatment should be applied for a fracture of the thigh.
11. Splinting should be attempted only when necessary to move the patient at once.
12. Traction should be applied to the limb below the fracture to permit moving without further injury and shock.
13. A special splint is necessary to provide traction.
14. When patient must be moved, carry him gently as short a distance as possible, pay special attention to the support of the injured limb in the extended position.
15. When the skull is fractured, medical attention must be obtained as soon as possible.
16. To prevent wound infection, a dressing must be applied.
17. For a fracture of the jaw, a triangular bandage or handkerchief is secured under the chin and over the top of the head.
18. For a fracture of the ribs, a wide band or several narrow bands of rubber plaster should be applied two-thirds around the chest, while the arms are held over the head and the chest emptied of air. Wide bandages should be applied around the chest, snugly.

SLINGS

1. The forearm should be supported by a sling when the forearm, upper arm and collarbone are fractured.
2. Bandages are usually used to make an arm sling.
3. Safety pins may be used to fasten the coat sleeve to the front of the coat to support the arm.
4. To support the arm, the coat flap should be pinned to the coat front or punch a hole in its lower edge and button it to a coat button.

COMBAT CONDITIONING PROGRAM

I. Drill:

1. Manual of Arms (5 minutes).
2. Close and Extended Order (15 minutes).
3. Physical Drill Under Arms (5 minutes).
   Stack Arms (3 minutes).

II. Accelerated Calisthenics—Stress Speed —No Rests.

1. Clap hands—running in place accelerate.
2. Side straddle hop hand slapping head — 16 counts. Rhythm — 16 counts—speed—men count.
3. Side straddle hop—hands on deck —16 counts. Rhythm—16 counts—speed—men count.
4. Breathing exercise—
   (a) Inhale — hold breath — pound chest with fists. Exhale.
      1. Repeat once.
   (b) Inhale—hold breath — hammer stomach with sides of hand — exhale.
      1. Repeat once.
5. Extend arms, touch alternate feet with opposite hand — stretch — 2 counts—16 counts—men count.
   (a) Bend extend arms—wind mill —16 counts — speed — men count.

6. Russian dance—arm bend—squat—left leg out—8 counts—right—8 counts—alternate—16 counts—latter—fast—shake legs out at finish.
7. Clasp hands under knees—shuffling feet—alternate 16 counts—rhythm—16 counts—fast.
8. Stoop sitting—hands between legs—left foot back 8 counts—right foot back—8 counts—both back 16 counts.
9. Grass drill—running in place—front go—back go—right go—left go—back go—front go.
10. Push ups—hands under chest—push up both hands and feet off deck—slap hands—catch self—let down—accelerate action.
11. Hands at side—heels six inches off deck—heels and hands out—back — accelerate action. Alternate with heels six inches off deck hammering stomach.
12. Rocking horse.
13. Bicycle exercise.
14. Alternate with rotating feet—stiff legged bringing heels close to ground—also sitting up slowly—back to prone slowly.
15. Heels and toes on deck alternately.
16. Hurdlers' exercise.

UP ON FEET

III. Contact—Pair Off:
1. Hand wrestling.
2. Lock back of necks—bulldogging.
3. Exchange hands on opponent's chest alternately—alternating feet.

4. Same except heels of hands in abdomen. Accelerate above.
5. Pushing exercise—drape arm over opponent's neck, one hand on deck—push.
6. Lock arms back to back—pull up—shake opponent.
7. Rooster fighting.
8. Fireman carry.

IV. Tumbling:

1. Forward somersault.
2. Backward somersault—knees high—run backward.
3. Side roll.
   (b) Alternate sides.
4. General warm-ups — on mat — stress recovery with hands up.

V. Hand to Hand Phase:

1. Chokes and breaks.
2. Wrist lock and breaks.
3. Arm grabs—go behind with leg sweep.
4. Hip throw.
5. All judo throws—slams.
6. Breaks for same.
7. Elbows—forearms—offensive use of same.
8. Kicks—stamps.
9. Pistol and knife—disarming.
10. Mass bare handed boxing.

VI. Club Routine.

VII. Bayonet Drill—new.
(b) Disarming.

VIII. Obstacle Course with Rifles and Bayonets.

IX. Rope Climbing.

X. Swimming routine when possible—IV, V, VI, VII, VIII, IX used alternately —stressing V, VI, VIII as troops progress.

NOTE: Swim program should include:
1. Tread water—proper breathing—variety of strokes.
2. Use of trousers — shirts as water wings.
3. Use of helmets—pails—tops of GI cans to keep one afloat.
4. Proper way to leave deck of sinking aircraft carrier or troopship.
5. Methods of swimming in water where oil is aflame.
6. Life saving methods:
   (a) Towing comrade.
   (b) Breaking desperation holds.
7. Resuscitation.

This Book Property of

NAME

ADDRESS

CITY   STATE

Printed in U.S.A.

A Selection Of Classic Instructive Titles Relating To The Art Of Pugilism & Self Defence In Both War & Peace
Find our entire selection @ naval-military-press.com

ALL-IN FIGHTING
The distilled knowledge of W.E. Fairbairn, legendary SOE instructor in unarmed combat, and inventor of the Sykes-Fairbairn knife, who learned his deadly skills in 30 years on the Shanghai waterfront.
Fully illustrated.
9781847348531

ART OF BOXING AND SCIENCE OF SELF DEFENCE
Former Lightweight Champion Billy Edwards shares the techniques and strategies of the sweet science in his beautifully illustrated boxing guide. Explore boxing's transition from bare knuckle spectacle to today's Marquis of Queensbury ruleset.
9781474539548

SELF DEFENCE OR THE ART OF BOXING
Ned Donnelly was a pioneer of boxing training during the late Victorian era. Explore the strategies and techniques used by this trainer of champions via a series of easy-to-follow illustrations and clear, concise coaching steps.
9781474539562

JACK GOODWIN'S BOXING

This 1920's boxing masterpiece by Jack Goodwin puts you in the shoes of a coach in that era. Uncover the best ways to run, manage and train boxers as taught by Jack Goodwin, a champion and trainer of champions in the noble science.

9781474539586

ART OF WRESTLING

George de Relwyskow Army Gymnastic Staff

In the appreciation to this book Captain Daniels, V.C., M.C., Rifle Brigade, states: "In adding a word to this book on the style of wrestling as taught at the Headquarters Gymnasium of the British Army, and having had personal experience in the various holds and throws taught, I consider it has been of great value in the training of the soldier, and the bringing out of those qualities of grit and determination which have been seen in all ranks who have taken an active part throughout the greatest war in history." 1919.

9781783313563

THE COMPLETE BOXER

Gunner Moir provides detailed instructions on the techniques he deployed to become British Heavyweight Champion. Taught in a series of easy to learn techniques, combinations, and boxing strategies.

9781474539609

KILL OR GET KILLED
Rex Applegate's "kill or be killed" helped prepare America's marines, soldiers, sailors, spies and airmen for the realities of war. This highly shared and respected work provides all you need to know about unarmed combat and close quarter engagement with the enemy.
9781474539661

BOXING (V-Five)
The Aviation Training Office of the Chief of Naval Operations
The game-changing V-Five suite of training manuals helped get a generation of American aviators fit for war. Here we explore how the airmen of the US navy trained in boxing as part of their military fitness regime.
9781474539623

THE TEXTBOOK OF WRESTLING
Get your wrestling skills matt-ready from wrestling champion and world-renown trainer Ernest Gruhn. Replete with detailed holds, throws, pins and strategies for success in a wide range of wrestling rulesets.
9781474539647

MANUAL OF PHYSICAL TRAINING 1914
(United States Army)
Published just prior to the outbreak of World War 1, this beautifully illustrated guide was designed to revolutionise the combat fitness and readiness of the US Army covering a wide range of gymnastic and combat calisthenic exercises.
9781474539708

DEAL THE FIRST DEADLY BLOW
United States Department of the Army

This Vietnam-era classic showcases in detail how the US Forces trained in close quarter combat. Known as the "encyclopaedia of combat" it helped a generation learn how to become devastating effective with empty hands, knives and bayonets alike.

9781474539722

HAND-TO-HAND COMBAT
Bureau of Aeronautics U.S Navy 1943

This is one of the best combative manuals from World War 2, developed by the US Navy V-Five Staff, that included the renowned American wrestler Wesley Brown. It is then not especially surprising that wrestling skills predominate in this manual, and form the base skill-set for this combative system.

9781474537391

ABWEHR ENGLISCHER GANGSTER METHODEN DEFENSE OF ENGLISH GANGSTERS METHODS – SILENT KILLING – FULL ENGLISH TRANSLATION

In 1942 the Wehrmacht published a training manual with the goal of countering the "silent killing" tactics used by the British commando units. The manual was – much in line with typical National Socialist terminology –titled

"Abwehr Englischer Gangster-methoden" or "Defence Against English Gangster methods".

This book was compiled due the Wehrmacht intelligence operatives uncovering of a British hand-to-hand course for the SOE, Commandos, et al, on methods of quick and silent killing (undoubtedly developed by W. E. Fairbairn and E. A. Sykes). They correctly assessed that their troops in general and particularly the Geheime Staatspolizei (Gestapo), Sicherheitsdienst (SD), their security guards, and sentries would be in grave danger when confronted by men trained in these methods. This manual/program was the Wehrmacht's response.

9781474538336

HAND TO HAND COMBAT

Francois d'Eliscu taught thousands of U.S. Army Rangers how to fight down and dirty in World War II.d'Eliscu doesn't get the press that Fairbairn and Applegate do, but he did a commendable job writing this book.It is basic, meant for training raw recruits in a short amount of time before sending them to the front, but simple is good when you are in combat, as most combative experts' will tell you.

9781474535823

WE Fairbairn's Complete Compendium of Lethal, Unarmed, Hand-to-Hand Combat Methods and Fighting In Colour

All 844 images of Fairbairn and his assistants can now for the first time be seen in full colour, lending a clarity to the practical methods of mastering the manner of dealing with an assailant, both in time of war and when placed in difficulty during unpleasant modern urban situations. These various holds, trips, kicks, blows etc, allow the average man or woman a position of security against almost any form of armed or unarmed attack.

Captain W.E. Fairbairn would have approved of this new colour version, that gives an illustrative clarity to the original that was lacking in previous monochrome reprints of his work.

All six of W.E. Fairbairn's works in one binding to create the ultimate colour compendium: Get Tough-All-In Fighting-Shooting to Live-Scientific Self-Defence-Hands Off!-Defend

9781783318735

BOXING FOR BOYS
Regtl. Sergt.-Major E B Dent Army Gymnastic Headquarters

A successful system of boxing instruction for large classes, to allow tuition with no detriment to the "backward or shy pupil". Covers Kit-On, Guard-Sparring-Advance-Point & Mark-Ducking-Medicine, Bag-Left & Right Hooks etc. The author considered that boxing systematically taught to the youth was beneficial exercise, and would have a marked elevating influence on the national character.

9781783314607

HAND-TO-HAND FIGHTING
A System Of Personal Defence For The Soldier (1918)

A tough book on the art of hand to hand fighting in the trenches of the Great War. Demonstrating techniques utilised to "do away with the enemy", many of which are barred in clean wrestling, the book includes good clear photographic illustrations presenting important attack methods including the "Hammer Lock", "Kidney Kick", "Head Twist", "Knee Groin Kick", and the "Knee Break", all very important in a man to man, life or death encounter, when fighting in the mud of the trenches.

9781783313983

COLD STEEL

A cold-war combatives classic. John Styers, US Marine and WW2 veteran, lays out his approach to close quarters combat with rifle, bayonet, stick, knife and empty hands. Explore what helped wartime and post-war Marines stay ahead of the competition with lucid imagery and clear combative descriptions.

9781474540643

THE COMPLETE KANO JIU-JITSU

Join world-famous physical culture expert H. Irving Hancock, and Jiu-Jitsu specialist Katsukama Higashi as they showcase the art of 'Kano Jiu-Jitsu' now known as Judo. Get an exclusive glimpse into the transitional era of the martial art, alongside how it uses Japanese physical culture methodologies for self-improvement.

9781474540735

SCIENTIFIC UNARMED COMBAT
The Art of Dynamic Self-Defence

Learn the esoteric Sri Lankan art of 'Cheena-Adi' with R. A Vairamuttu. This guide explores armed and unarmed self-defence drawing heavily from Indian martial culture, alongside wellness and development from Indian physical culture, fitness, diet and medicine.

9781474540728

SELF DEFENCE FOR WOMEN
COMBATO

Join the Canadian combatives legend William "Bill" Underwood as he showcases self-defence for women. Over the course of clear photography, sketches and instructions he lays out a curriculum for self-defence for the attacks women would be most likely to face.

9781474540711

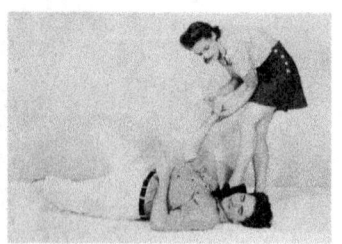

THE NEW SCIENCE
Weaponless Defence

Join wrestling champions Prof F. S Lewis, William V Gregory and Boxing Champ Tommy Burns as they showcase street orientated self-defence from people with a proven track record of fighting success. This 1906 manual via a series of photos and instructions lays out simple, tried and tested ways to keep yourself safe.

9781474540704

COMBAT CONDITIONING MANUAL
Jiu-Jitsu Defence, Bayonet Defence and Club Defence

This 1942 guide for marines lays out the basics of combat Ju Jitsu as part of an overall training regimen for US Marines. It's a holistic guide that covers defences against armed and unarmed attackers, physical fitness and even first aid.

9781474540698

BOXING TAUGHT THROUGH "SLOW MOTION FILM"

Learn the ropes from the best fighters of the 1900s-1930s in this unique boxing manual. Using stills from super slow-mo fight footage, this treasure trove unpacks the skills, tips and tactics of the champs for you to emulate at home.

9781474540681

HOW TO BOX CORRECTLY

Explore the art of boxing according to famous Bronx boxing brand Ben Lee in this 1944 how-to guide. Learn the ropes from one of the nation's top trainers and boxing journalists John J. Romano, in this warmly illustrated guide to the sweet science.

9781474540674

www.ingramcontent.com/pod-product-compliance
Lightning Source LLC
LaVergne TN
LVHW051507070426
835507LV00022B/2967